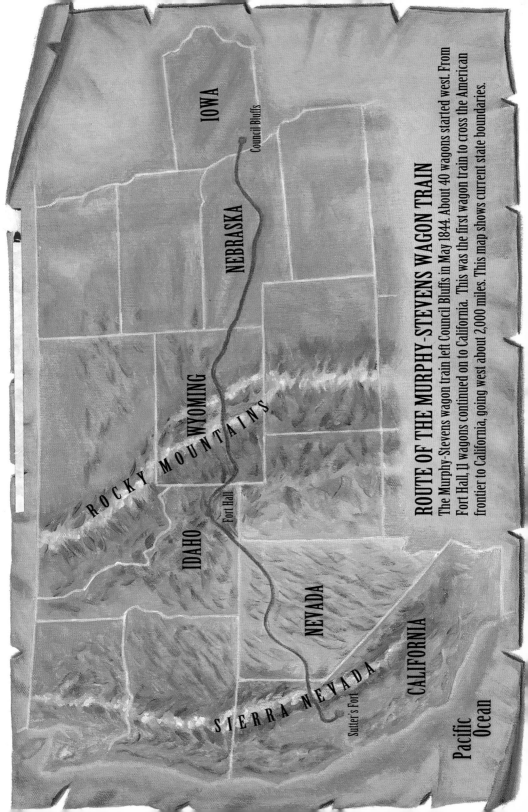

ROUTE OF THE MURPHY-STEVENS WAGON TRAIN

The Murphy-Stevens wagon train left Council Bluffs in May 1844. About 40 wagons started west. From Fort Hall, 11 wagons continued on to California. This was the first wagon train to cross the American frontier to California, going west about 2,000 miles. This map shows current state boundaries.

IOWA

Council Bluffs

NEBRASKA

WYOMING

R O C K Y   M O U N T A I N S

Fort Hall

IDAHO

NEVADA

SIERRA NEVADA

Sutter's Fort

CALIFORNIA

Pacific
Ocean

Seeking Adventure

1844

Moses Schallenberger was 17
and ready for adventure.
His sister, Elizabeth, and her husband
were moving to California.
Moses was going with them.
Going west in a wagon train
would certainly be exciting.

4

The pioneers left Iowa Territory in May.
They began to cross the prairie.
Moses drove the oxen that pulled
his sister's wagon.
He and his friends, Joseph and Allen,
helped hunt buffalo and antelope.
They took turns guarding the oxen
at night.

In October, Moses looked up at the tallest

mountains he had ever seen.

The wagon train had come 2,000 miles

in six months.

Snow was falling.

The pioneers were cold and wet.

They were low on supplies.

Their tired oxen needed grass to eat,

or they would die.

A big, warm valley lay

on the western side of the mountains.

It was 100 miles away.

Before winter set in, the pioneers had to

reach that part of California.

Moses helped look for a way
through the mountains.
It had to be wide enough for a wagon
and a team of oxen.
But the pioneers could not find a pass.
The oxen began to die.
Moses helped empty six of the wagons.
The pioneers pulled them up
rock walls with chains and ropes.
They led the oxen up and over
narrow mountain trails.
More snow fell.

One group set out for Sutter's Fort.
They had to leave
most of their belongings behind.
When they reached Sutter's Fort,
they would send back help.
Another group went ahead
on horseback.
Elizabeth joined them.

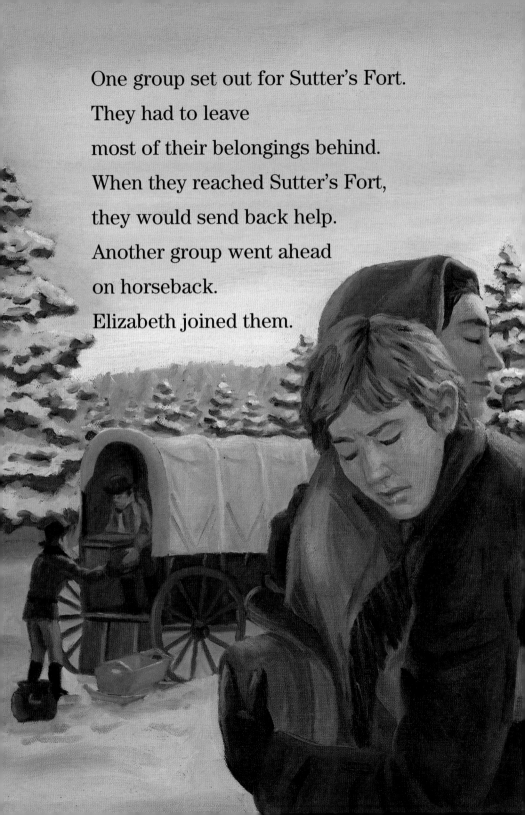

Moses hugged his sister.
It was hard to say good-bye.
Moses and his friends,
Joseph and Allen, stayed behind.
They would guard the belongings.
They built a log cabin
and put everything inside.

Blinding-white snow covered everything,
even the wagons.

Moses and his friends tried to hunt.

But some of the wild animals were
hibernating in dens under the snow.

Others had migrated away for the winter.

The three friends decided to hike
over the mountains
before they starved to death.
They could not wait for help.
They quickly made snowshoes
and packed dried beef.
It was the only food they had.

Escape

Late November 1844

Moses, Joseph, and Allen left
the next morning.
It was hard to walk in the soft snow!
Moses's legs ached.
His snowshoes did not fit well.
Soon his muscles knotted in pain.
But he could not stop.
Like his friends,
Moses was eager to escape the snow.
They had to reach safety!
Steep rock walls lay ahead,
and there was deep snow everywhere.
Somehow, Moses had to climb
those walls.
A crow flew by,
and Moses wished for wings.

With every step, Moses groaned.

He tried not to think about his legs.

He climbed slowly.

He was cold and out of breath.

Frosty air stung his throat.

He stopped.

He had to rest.

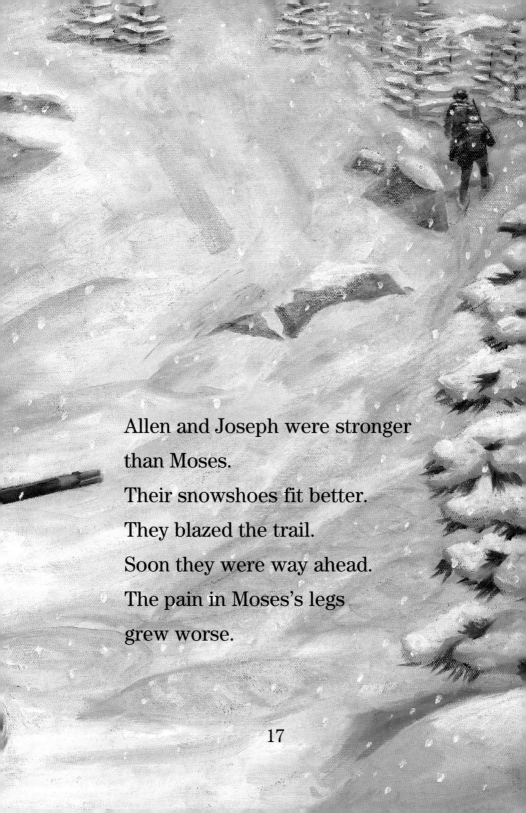

Allen and Joseph were stronger
than Moses.
Their snowshoes fit better.
They blazed the trail.
Soon they were way ahead.
The pain in Moses's legs
grew worse.

That night, they camped in the snow.

Even with a fire,

they were freezing cold.

In the morning, Moses was stiff.

Allen helped him stand up.

Sharp pain raced down Moses's legs

and into his feet.

If Allen and Joseph had to wait

for Moses, they might not reach

Sutter's Fort.

Moses had only one choice.

He strapped on his pack.

He picked up his rifle.

The three friends shook hands.

And Moses turned around.

Moses did not look back.

It would be too hard.

His pack felt heavy.

So did his heart.

Step-by-step,

he followed the snowshoe tracks back.

He staggered through the snow all day.

His legs hurt.

His eyes watered from the pain.

Just before dark,
Moses reached the cabin.
It was cold and dark inside.
He started a fire in the fireplace.
Then he fell fast asleep.

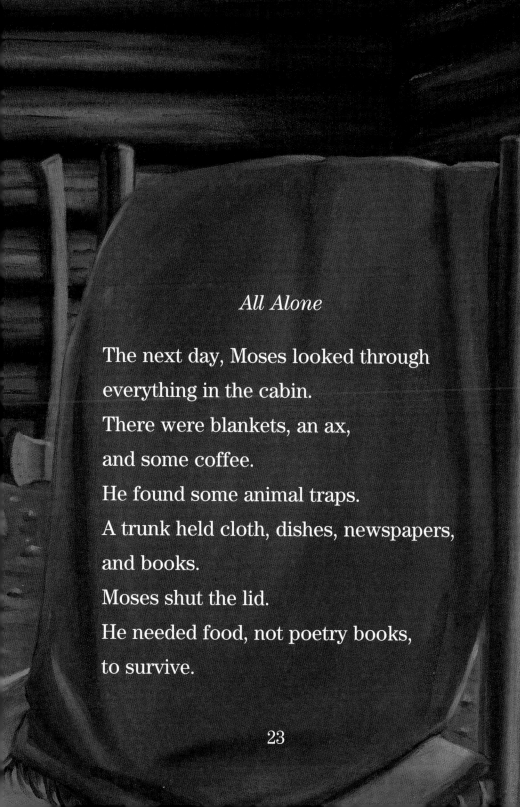

All Alone

The next day, Moses looked through
everything in the cabin.
There were blankets, an ax,
and some coffee.
He found some animal traps.
A trunk held cloth, dishes, newspapers,
and books.
Moses shut the lid.
He needed food, not poetry books,
to survive.

Moses set two traps near the cabin.

His legs still hurt,

and he worried he would fall.

The temperature was dropping.

The tip of Moses's nose began to sting.

It would be easy to get frostbite.

Moses gathered some broken-off
tree branches.
Inside, he added them to the fire.
Soon the fire warmed the cabin.
Moses's stomach growled.
He was hungry, very hungry.

Finally, Moses caught an old, thin coyote
in one of the traps.
Using his knife,
he skinned off the coyote's fur.
He roasted the meat.
It smelled delicious.
But it tasted terrible.
Moses felt sick to his stomach.
Maybe coyote meat would be better
stewed slowly.
So Moses boiled it in a pot.
It still tasted bad.
Moses pretended
it was tender buffalo steak.
He ate more, very slowly.

Moses trapped two foxes.

He cooked and ate one fox.

The meat was tasty!

Moses was still hungry.

But he had to be smart to survive,
so he saved one fox.

He ate half of the fox the next day.

He finished it the day after.

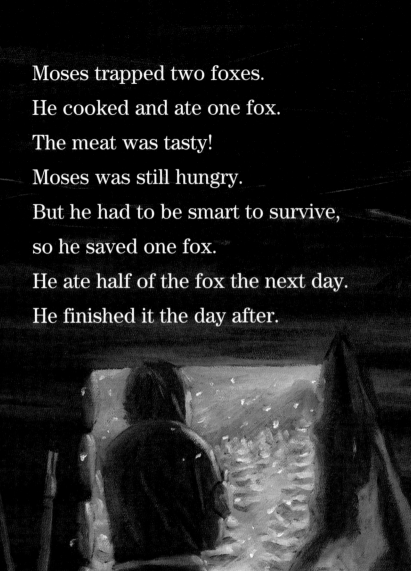

Every day, Moses looked
at the mountains.
When he got stronger,
he would walk west again.
This time, he would not fail!
First, he needed a good supply of food.
Second, he needed a long break
between storms.

One morning,
when Moses checked his traps,
he found a fox that was still alive.
It wiggled.
As Moses rushed forward,
the fox slipped free.
Moses chased it.
He had to catch that fox!

Moses fell into an icy-cold creek.

Using all his strength, he crawled out.

His rifle had landed on the snow.

It was dry, but his clothes were wet.

Moses shivered.

He hurried inside and undressed.

Wrapped in a blanket,

Moses warmed himself.

He sipped coffee.

Finally, his teeth stopped chattering.

He was lucky to be alive.

For many days, the wind howled.

More snow fell,

nearly burying the cabin.

Moses paced back and forth.

He was lonely.

He was hungry and scared.

Maybe he should leave a letter

for his sister.

What if she found his bones

in the spring?

Moses opened the trunk
and searched for writing paper.
Instead, he found newspapers
and books.
Even though the news was old,
he read the newspapers.
Then he opened one of the poetry books.
By firelight,
Moses began to read a poem out loud.
His own voice calmed him.
He forgot to write his sister.

Each night, Moses pulled out

his hunting knife.

He cut a notch in a log near the door

to keep track of the time.

Moses finished the coffee

on Christmas Day.

He thought about Elizabeth.

They had always spent Christmas together.

Outside, the winter wind roared.

Inside, Moses recited a poem.

Now he knew many poems

from memory.

New Year's Day came and went.

Moses counted more than 30 notches.

He had lived alone for over a month.

It seemed like forever!

His hair was as messy

as a squirrel's nest.

His clothes smelled.

Finally, in February, there were breaks
between snowstorms.
The temperature dropped,
and the top of the snow froze hard.
Moses could walk on the snow.
As soon as the storm clouds were gone,
he would leave his white prison.

One afternoon, Moses thought he saw

a person far away.

He rubbed his eyes.

A man *was* walking toward him!

It was Dennis Martin

from the wagon train.

He had come back to rescue Moses.

Tears filled Moses's eyes.

They hugged each other.

Dennis brought food *and* good news!

Moses's sister, Elizabeth, was safe

at Sutter's Fort.

So was everyone else

in the wagon train.

Moses begged Dennis to keep talking.

He had waited three months to hear

another voice.

It was a beautiful sound!

Crossing the Mountains
March 1845

The next morning, Moses and Dennis
started for the wall of mountains.
Only once did Moses look back.
He saw the cabin.
Eleven frozen coyotes were nailed
to one wall.
He would never eat one again!
The two men climbed higher
and higher.
The snow was deep.
Icy-cold wind blasted them.
Soon they reached a narrow pass.
Storm clouds swirled.
But they hurried on.

Moses and Dennis began
to hike downhill.
Spring had arrived on the west side
of the mountains.
Animals grazed on new grass.
Fish swam in a nearby river.
There was plenty of food here!

Ahead, Moses saw a wide valley
and Sutter's Fort.
A dirt road led into the big fort.
Two doors stood open.
People, animals, and wagons
were coming and going.
Moses hurried inside.
How would he find Elizabeth?

Across the grounds,

Moses saw a woman waving at him.

She ran so fast

her bonnet blew off her head.

It was Elizabeth!

Moses ran too.

Brother and sister hugged.

They cried.

Moses's long, lonely months were over.

Afterword

Moses Schallenberger was part of the Murphy-Stevens (or Murphy-Stephens) wagon train, which left Council Bluffs, Iowa Territory, in 1844. It was the first wagon train to reach California by going over the Sierra Nevada, a high mountain range in the West.

In November 1846, the wagon train of another group, the Donner Party, reached the eastern side of the Sierra Nevada. It snowed and snowed. Like Moses, the Donner Party was trapped. They put up tents. They built more cabins near a small lake, now called Donner Lake. One family used Moses's cabin. The Donner Party did not have enough food to survive the winter. The party was rescued in 1847, but some people had already died.

Moses spent the rest of his life in California. His sister, Elizabeth, and her husband died in a cholera epidemic in 1850. Moses raised their infant son. That same year, California became the 31st state in the United States.

For the rest of his life, Moses and his wife, Fannie, and their five children lived on a farm in San Jose, California. When he was an old man, Moses dictated his survival story to his daughter, Margaret. He died in 1909 at the age of 82.

Moses's story took place near Donner Lake and the present-day town of Truckee, California. It is one of the snowiest places in the world.

Further Reading

BOOKS

Calabro, Marian. *The Perilous Journey of the Donner Party.* New York: Clarion Books, 1999. This is a gripping account of the Donner Party's 1846–1847 trek from Illinois to California. Read about the weather conditions and personality conflicts that kept the pioneers stranded in the mountains for the winter.

Freedman, Russell. *Children of the Wild West.* New York: Clarion Books, 1983. Find out more about daily life in the Wild West, through the eyes of children who lived there.

Lavender, David. *Snowbound: The Tragic Story of the Donner Party.* New York: Holiday House, 1996. This book gives a detailed telling of the Donner Party's disastrous journey.

Russell, Marion. *Along the Santa Fe Trail: Marion Russell's Own Story.* Adapted by Ginger Wadsworth. Morton Grove, IL: Albert Whitman & Company, 1993. This book tells a seven-year-old's story of her journey west in a wagon train.

Stewart, George. *The Opening of the California Trail.* Berkeley, CA: University of California Press, 1953. You can read Moses Schallenberger's own words, based on his memoirs, in this book.

Wadsworth, Ginger. *Words West, Voices of Young Pioneers.* New York: Clarion Books, 2004. Read stories of children who traveled west in wagon trains, in their own words.

WEBSITES

Donner Memorial State Park
http://www.parks.ca.gov/?page_id=503
Learn more about the area and about Moses Schallenberger and the Donner Party. The park and museum are popular stopping places for people from all over the world.

Forgotten Journey: Opening the California Trail Experience
http://thecaliforniatrail.com/who.asp
This website supplements a movie titled *Forgotten Journey.* Short bios of pioneers on the Murphy-Stevens wagon train and links to teacher guides and maps are included.